# Remembering the WAR

## *Years* and *After*

# Remembering the WAR
## Years
### and
# After

KIM WARREN

# REMEMBERING THE WAR YEARS AND AFTER

*iUniverse books may be ordered through booksellers or by contacting:*

*iUniverse*
*1663 Liberty Drive*
*Bloomington, IN 47403*
*www.iuniverse.com*
*1-800-Authors (1-800-288-4677)*

*Because of the dynamic nature of the Internet, any web addresses or links contained in this book may have changed since publication and may no longer be valid. The views expressed in this work are solely those of the author and do not necessarily reflect the views of the publisher, and the publisher hereby disclaims any responsibility for them.*

*Any people depicted in stock imagery provided by Thinkstock are models, and such images are being used for illustrative purposes only. Certain stock imagery © Thinkstock.*

*ISBN: 978-1-4917-8998-8 (sc)*
*ISBN: 978-1-4917-8999-5 (e)*

*Library of Congress Control Number: 2016902471*

*Print information available on the last page.*

*iUniverse rev. date: 2/17/2016*

Map of Canada

Map of Europe and Egypt

*To those who lived and to those who did not.*

# CONTENTS

# PREFACE

In October, 2013, I attended my high school reunion in Montreal. It was a weekend event which allowed for ample time to chat with classmates whom I had not seen in a very long time.

While helping to put agendas together on Saturday morning, Harry Teitelbaum told me about his father's escape from France during WWII. The next day, over lunch, Garry Kallos spoke with me about his parents. They were from Hungary and had survived the Holocaust.

Forty years ago, as teenagers this was something we never talked about. Now maturity had brought with it a different level of conversation. I was deeply moved as I listened to what they had to say.

The idea of writing their stories in a book occurred to me. I asked them what they thought of this and they were open to it. So the writing began.

I put out a request to see if other classmates would share their stories. Ghislaine Bochi, Susan Grodan and Henry Cohen responded. Henry introduced me to Yvette Beza, his aunt by marriage, who lives in Greece.

Although not a classmate, Jacques Mydlarski also spoke with me.

Initially the book was to be about my Jewish friends whose families had survived the holocaust. As time went on it seemed like the book began to take on a life of its own. I was being drawn to people who had a story to tell and though they are not Jewish, the war time accounts of Una Barrett, Evertje Kroes, and Helen Skawinski are included. I decided to also convey my mothers' family story, the Field's.

Thinking the book to finally be finished, it turned out otherwise. A conversation with two sisters, Henrietta Pente and Margaret Graham, gave insight into what they had gone through.

Being an avid reader I had read many stories of people that survived the war. I often wondered what happened to them post war. Where did they go? What did they do? Where possible I answer those questions.

Writing this book was not easy. As I interviewed people I sensed that reliving the past was very difficult for them. Despite the years the memories were still painful to remember.

For me, as I transcribed the tapes from the interviews, there were many times when I had to step away as I was overcome with emotion. I struggled with the loss of life and how humanity could do what it did to itself.

# ACKNOWLEDGEMENTS

Sincerest thanks to Harry, Garry, Ghislaine, Susan, Henry, Yvette, Jacques, Una, Evertje, Helen, Henrietta and Margaret and their families who spent many hours talking with me.

My cousins Mark and his wife Nanette, Stephen and the cousins in England, thank you for all that you shared. Nanette, an author in her own right, was invaluable for her advice.

Moshe Dalva, another classmate from high school, offered feedback and encouragement.

Adrienne Bladon assisted with the photos.

Mary Lee Wagoner helped with proof reading.

My deepest appreciation goes to Una, for giving wings to this book.

# INTRODUCTION

It is said that one person can change the course of history. When it came to World War II that person was Adolph Hitler. His actions and beliefs and those of his followers changed the lives and futures for millions of innocent people. They did not ask for the emotional trauma or brutality that they experienced. They did not choose death but were not given a choice.

"Remembering The War Years and After" is a collection of stories about what families experienced during Hitler's reign of terror. While some fled and others hid, both were dependant on the kindness of people to help them. Families were torn apart, forcibly taken to work as slave labourers in Germany or deported to concentration camps where they were killed, or lived a meager existence not knowing if they would survive one day to the next. There was also the fear of bombs being dropped on them which became part of their daily existence.

Food, a basic necessity of life was limited and often hard to find or withheld. Starvation loomed bringing with it death.

It would seem as if the world had gone mad and no one was stopping a mad man. There were those who tried to put an end to it. Risking their lives they volunteered to fight the evil that had threatened to take over the world.

When the war finally ended, what became of the families? Some remained in their home countries to try and rebuild their lives and others chose to leave and start a new life. Thus their journey is a part of their story.

# CHAPTER ONE

## Fighting the Enemy

Henry and Ada Field lived in Saint-Henri, a working class neighbourhood in Montreal's west end. They had two daughters, Adeline and Irene and a younger son James. Their home was a triplex row house with outdoor staircases.

As the French and English lived side by side, Henry and his children were bilingual. Ada, who was from England, spoke only English. She stayed home to raise the children while Henry worked.

Teenagers Adeline and Irene left school early as money was needed to support the family. Adeline worked in accounting and Irene was a secretary.

Canada declared war on Nazi Germany on September 10, 1939. It joined Britain and France, which had done so several days earlier.

The Montreal Civilian Protection Committee was organized in 1939. Irene said, "I signed up with the Civil Defense and was issued an ID card, a helmet and a uniform." Part of her job was to make sure that the blackout rules were followed in case of a threat of invasion. At night she carried a flashlight and went around checking houses looking for any signs of light, which meant that the blackout curtains were not closed properly.

Many war industries were located in Montreal. Irene and Adeline had been working at the Robert Mitchell Company. In 1942, the business began producing brass cartridge case munition.

As Canada was sending a lot of food overseas and the military also required large amounts, rationing became necessary. It began in January of 1942 and Henry and Ada had to manage. Ration books were given to householders.

In the beginning sugar, tea and coffee were limited as they were imported products. The merchant ships that brought these goods were needed in the war effort. Furthermore many of the vessels had been sunk by German U-boats. Being tea drinkers Ada and Henry had to cut back, and as sugar was also needed in the production of shells and bombs, limiting its availability even further, they had less to add to their tea.

Rationing of gasoline started in April. The family did not have a car so that was not as important to them. Living in a large city they could rely on the streetcars. Come December, butter was included.

In May of 1943 meat was added and two pounds per week, per person was the limit. It was an essential ingredient in their meals so the shortage of it was felt. December of that year, the list grew with the addition of molasses, apple and honey butters, maple syrup, canned fruit and evaporated milk. By 1944 there would be cheese, canned blueberries, pie filling, and beer as well.

Silk stockings, another imported item, were rare to acquire. Irene being a fashionable young woman said, "I painted my legs with make-up and drew a seam line with a make-up pencil on the back of my legs so it would look as if I was wearing stockings. I always hoped it would not rain and wash my stockings away."

Although ships on the St. Lawrence Seaway were attacked by submarines as far as Quebec City and there were rumours of Germans getting off their ships and going to bars to try to gain military information the Field's experienced a milder war in Montreal than their relatives in England.

Ada had come over from England, by ship, just before the start of World War I. Her mother and sisters were still there. The threat of invasion was more imminent as they lived in Brighton, Sussex along the south coast.

Sussex was to be a front line of defense and heavy artillery lined the seafronts. The beaches Ada had once gone to were now mined and guarded with barbed wire. The piers she had strolled on had sections removed so they could not be used as a landing place for the enemy.

Identity cards and gas masks were issued. Once night fell a blackout was enforced. No street lighting or house lights were to be seen. A curfew was in place from 6pm to 7am.

Ada worried about the safety of her family and indeed she had good reason to. Even though Brighton was not their main target, German bombers dropped whatever bombs they had left over after bombing London, on the place. In addition hit-and run-raids by bombers occurred and civilians walking along the streets were also strafed with machine gun fire. The "Brighton Blitz", took place between July 1940 and February 1944.

Ada's nephew, Edward (Ted), was in the Royal Navy. Ted's duty with his ship was in the Atlantic Ocean where the waters could be deadly from German U-boat attacks. Ted said, "In 1943 the bow of my ship was torpedoed and had to be dry docked in Newfoundland for repairs. I felt my work was risky and not wanting to make anyone a widow, I made a promise to myself not to marry during the war."

Her niece Freda worked with Polish flyers on R and R. Freda met her husband during the course of this work and her first encounter with him was far from romantic. Freda recalled, "James, a Canadian soldier, boldly entered the room I was in and bellowed at me, "Get those blackout curtains closed." I instantly disliked him." Over time a love grew and they married in 1943, he wearing his uniform and she a simple frock.

Henry, having been a Canadian soldier with the Black Watch in World War I, knew the atrocities of war. He had been seriously wounded and his brother, Joseph, had died when they were fighting in France.

Their father and uncle had immigrated to Canada but the remainder of the family lived in Canterbury, in the south east of England.

Canterbury, well known culturally for its cathedral, was close to Luftwaffe airfields in occupied France and was bombed numerous times. Fighter aircraft also opened fire on people in the streets. It was part of the "Baedeker Raids" in 1942 which resulted in major destruction. The main body of the cathedral escaped damage due to fire watchers stationed up on the roof throwing incendiary bombs off but the library was destroyed.

In an attempt to weaken the British into submission, U-boats attacked ships carrying supplies of food and other goods to them. As a result Henry's family had to endure rationing that began in 1940. Every person received an identity card, a ration book and coupons. Butter, sugar, eggs, meat and tinned goods, as well as gasoline, clothes and furniture were all rationed.

Cousin Frieda said, "I was a first time mum with a baby born at the beginning of the war. I greatly welcomed food packages sent from Montreal by my cousins, Beryl and Emma who were sisters." Inside the parcels were tinned goods, chocolate bars, jams and other items which were much needed.

In his early twenties, another cousin, Leslie, had joined the Royal Air Force. The RAF was unable to train their pilots in Britain because of the possibility of enemy attack, unpredictable weather and the strain caused by wartime traffic at airfields. So, they sent them to various Commonwealth countries as part of The British Commonwealth Air Training Plan. Leslie said, "I was sent to RAF Thornhill in Rhodesia to train."

Back in Canada, cousins James and Frances (Bud) had enlisted in 1939 in Winnipeg where they lived.

Jim, as James liked to be called, signed up with the Royal Canadian Air Force. The RCAF sent him a letter of acceptance. His mother, Alice, had other ideas. When the letter arrived she was the first to read it. Remembering what her husband, Frank, had gone through while fighting in WWI, she promptly ripped it up and said, "My sons won't be cannon fodder." Jim, thinking he had been rejected by the RCAF, enlisted as an infantry soldier in the Canadian army. He served with the Cameron Highlanders. It was only much later that he learned what his mother had done.

Like his brother Jim, Bud enlisted as an infantry man.

After training in Britain for years, both brothers were sent with their units as reinforcements to Normandy after D-Day in 1944. The objective for the Canadian military was to clear the coasts of France, Belgium, the Netherlands and Germany.

Jim, wounded in the upper body by shrapnel, was evacuated to England for surgery and to recuperate. In all likelihood his injuries meant he would be sent back to Canada. At the hospital he was asked, "Would you be willing to volunteer and participate in an experimental drug trial that could help you heal faster?" Jim replied, "Yes." The drug turned out to be penicillin and with its efficient results he returned to fighting with his unit in Northwestern Europe.

Bud was also asked if he would volunteer, but for a different reason. The call came, "Does anyone have any motorcycle experience?" Bud said, "Figuring it would be better than fighting as an infantry man and having some knowledge of motorcycles, I signed up." At the time he did not know how dangerous this would be. His riding was done at nighttime and he could not use his headlights. Unable to see who was there, the sound of his motorcycle made him a target for snipers from both the German and Canadian armies. Bud commented, "Not being able to see where I was going, I repeatedly crashed into all the canals in Belgium and the Netherlands."

With the end of the war in 1945, Jim's war also ended in May in northern Germany on the Baltic coast when the Canadians met the Russians. Bud had also survived but would later require his hips to be replaced due to his jarring rides on the motorcycle. Both men had been away from home for six long years. After their return to Canada, Bud in 1945 and Jim in 1946, they married and settled back into life.

Freda travelled in 1946 by ship with other war brides to join her husband in Canada. Arriving in Halifax, she continued her journey by train to join James in Vancouver. Her brother, Edward (Ted), kept his promise and married after the war.

In 1946, Leslie married. He trained to be a school teacher at Goldsmith College in London, England. In the mid 1950's he took his wife and three sons to live in Welo, Rhodesia.

Irene received a certificate after the war for her work with the Civil Defense. It thanked her for her help in the "war against the German Reich and other Axis Powers."

Rationing in Canada continued until 1946. As factories and farmland in Europe had been destroyed Canada sent meat and other food items overseas as emergency aid.

In 1949 when Irene sailed to England to meet Ada's family, she brought a package containing beef with her. Kept in the ships cooler for the duration of the sailing, she arrived in Liverpool with her precious cargo. The beef was a welcomed gift as rationing did not end in England until July, 1954.

In the 1950's Irene married and had two children. Her husband's stepfather, Charles Rector, had been in the Merchant Navy during the war. He perished in June, 1942 when his ship, the S.S. Western Head, was torpedoed and sunk by U-107 in the Caribbean.

1943 – Wedding of Freda and James Rhoades.

Jim Field -WWII

# CHAPTER TWO

## Fear of the Bombs

U na Jarvis lived in Dartford, England with her parents William and Ethel Jarvis. She had two brothers, Lester, who was five years older and Alan, three and a half years older. Another sibling, Beryl, had passed away when she was five days old due to malnourishment.

Dartford, in the county of Kent, was bordered to the north by the Thames Estuary. It was both a marketing and industrial town. Two large companies were located in the downtown area, J & E Hall, builders of escalators and large trucks and, Burroughs Wellcome & Company, a medical/chemical producer. Cement works, paper mills and a power station were nearby, close to the river.

William was a talented hand printer on silk materials. He worked for a silk printing company located in Crayford and commuted back and forth to work by bus. The family had a hard time in the early 1930's during the Depression as the company closed down. The product was considered a luxury item and thus there were no markets for it. However in 1934 it reopened and William was able to return to work. They had a very pleasant life, although considered lower/middle class.

They lived in the first of eight terraced houses on Sussex Road that they rented from Ethel's mother, Florence Hicks. The house had two rooms with a little kitchen downstairs and two main bedrooms upstairs. The toilet was outside and bathing was done in a large portable tub placed in front of the dining room fire. In 1936 they moved to a semi-detached house just around the corner on the same street, which they rented from the builder.

Una began her schooling at York Road School when she was four and a half years old. It was located across the road from where they lived. She was not very happy during this time though. For six weeks in 1934 and for ten weeks in 1935 she had been hospitalized in the Bow Arrow Lane Isolation Hospital. Consequently, she recalls, "In those days, students were divided into A, B, and C classes and, needless to say, I was always in the C class."

Prior to the start of the war everyone was issued with a gas mask, in case the Germans used gas as they had done in the First World War. The mask was carried in a cardboard box with a shoulder strap. Babies up to a year old were protected by being placed in a soft container, so their head, arms and legs were safely inside for movement and the top was clear plastic for vision.

In September, 1939 when the war started, Una was ten years old. Like most mothers in those days, Ethel stayed home throughout the war. The unmarried women took the men's jobs in the factories and other places. Like other non-essential companies, William's silk printing company closed. He was assigned to work at the small engine factory, Beadles Limited, in Dartford, which manufactured items for sea planes. He remained there until after 1945.

At the beginning of the war all schools in Kent, Metropolitan London and other places of heavy manufacturing were closed because of the possibility of bombing. Most children were evacuated away from the danger to inland farming areas. Una was slated to join relatives in Canada, but the program was stopped after two ships carrying evacuees had been sunk by German U-boats in the Atlantic. Eight months later, after brick shelters were erected for protection on some of her schools' property, Una was able to attend classes two afternoons a week inside the shelters. She said, "I was armed with copious amounts of homework, which brought my grades up considerably."

In October the family moved again, this time to Florence Hicks' house. An aunt and an uncle had each married and, as houses were obviously not being built at that time, William and Ethel offered them the use of their house on Sussex Road.

Florence's house was just over a mile away on the corner of Great Queen Street and Gladstone Road. It was not attached to the other homes. The terraced houses across the street were built four feet higher. Consequently iron railings had been placed along the side walk for pedestrian safety. The railing ran from Fulwich Hill to twenty feet past the entrance to Gladstone Road.

She had a little corner shop on the main floor of her house and sold candies, cigarettes, biscuits, butter, eggs, and other items. It didn't have an actual name. It was just called, *Mrs. Hicks.* At the back of the store were a dining room, kitchen and scullery where a coal burning stove was the means of baking, along with a gas stove for regular cooking. Above there was a living room that had provided wonderful times at family parties but now it was where Lester and Alan slept. The two bedrooms were for Florence, who shared it with Una and the other for Ethel and William. A full bathroom was located at the top of the stairs.

In early 1940, Una was able to walk quite safely to school from her grandmother's house. However, the following year bombing occurred day and night as Dartford was a target due to its industry. On the south side of town, called the 'dark trees', and around a nearby small lake, little huts were built to give the appearance of local residents' allotments. This was to camouflage Vickers Armstrong, a large armament factory from enemy bombers. Fortunately, it was never bombed.

Una remembers several horrible times when the Germans started dropping Molotov cocktails that contained phosphorous. She said, "When they hit the ground the contents would splash and cause terrible burning. There were also oil bombs which caused fire upon explosion." In the first years of the war the bombs were small.

She recalls, "One awful night German bombers dropped an oil bomb five blocks up Great Queen Street from us. Another bomb fell in a farmer's field causing a hole about five feet in diameter. A bomb also fell in the back yard of the New Town Tavern pub taking down a brick wall that ran up the alley by the side of the homes across the street." The pub was located on the corner of Fulwich Hill.

The next day, the chief air raid warden came to inspect the wall. He said, "It is just a small bomb so everything is safe." As it was summer time the children were not at school, so Una and her friends played most of the day all around the area where the bomb had fallen.

Florence did not have a shelter. When the air raid siren went off at nine o'clock that night William took Una and Alan across the road to the pub's cellar for safety. Returning home he passed the broken wall, walked along the top side walk, crossed the road and entered the store.

At nine-twenty just as he was going into the door of the dining room a bomb went off. It was a delayed-action bomb which had fallen the previous night in the pub's backyard. It took out four of the houses across the street and the pub's garage. All the windows in the shop were blown out. The upstairs windows, where Lester and Alan would have been sleeping, tore their pillows to pieces from the glass shards. It was a miracle the bomb had not exploded when the children had been playing there earlier or while William was walking home. He literally made it to safety by a couple of minutes. Had he been delayed he would have been killed.

It was also very fortunate that everyone from the houses across the street had been in their Anderson shelters. The shelters, made of corrugated iron had been distributed to people to put in their back yards. Una said, "Gas was a means of lighting in those days. In a strange way that shows how a bomb blast can react, the gas jet on the bedroom wall of one of the houses that had been blown up was left with its fragile lace cover intact and still in place on the wall. Also a bed mattress from one of the homes landed in the garden of a house nearby."

In 1941 they returned to their home on Sussex Road. With rationing in place and as they had a very long backyard they grew fruit on one side and vegetables on the other. Ethel used the fruit to make jams and pies with her carefully saved sugar rations. As meat was also rationed, a neighbour, who managed a butcher shop, occasionally saved them some offal. He was also able to supply them with a sheep head which had a lot of meat on it, like tongue and cheeks. Ethel cooked it all up as a stew. Even the brain was used in dumplings, however Una exclaimed, "I would have mine plain!"

That year Una was able to return to school full time as a few of the children returned home, more teachers were available and daylight air raids were less frequent. Happily Una said, "During this time I met a new friend, Connie."

The Jarvis's did not have an Anderson shelter however they were friendly with the Draper family who lived in the row houses around the corner. When the raids were bad, Una took shelter there. At other times, if the attacks were extra heavy, she along with the other females in her house, including her Uncle Harold's wife Irene and their baby Valerie, took cover under the dining room table. In reality it could only shield them from flying glass.

There were nights in 1943, when the Jarvis's stood on their front door step and watched the ghastly glow of the fires raging in London. Sometimes they saw a German bomber caught in an anti-aircraft barrage streaking to the earth. The military also had large trucks armed with naval anti-aircraft guns, with which they would engage the attacking bombers. These trucks were kept mobile so they would not be caught stationary during an attack.

Connie and Una now attended Bexley Technical School. In addition to general education they took a secretarial course. The college was located eight miles nearer to London so Una went there by bus or on her bike. Una remembers, "During the war no-one was allowed to travel to London or anywhere else in Britain, unless they had a pass for work, government business or were military personnel."

Around the college, air raid shelters were dug into a small landscaped hill in the garden surrounding the building. Students could also go under the stage in the auditorium where typewriters were placed and they could continue their typing lessons. As the college was built just before the war, many windows surrounding the building had heavy webbing glued to the glass, in case of nearby explosions. Fortunately, none occurred.

Starting in June 1944 after Allied forces landed in Normandy, German V-1 rockets were fired at south-east England. They called them doodlebugs.

The morning after the V1's started, when William came home from his all-night duty as a Home Guard, Una asked him, "What's happening, the bombers are different?" He explained, "The noise is not from regular planes but are bombs with a rocket in the back and wings to glide them." Una remembers, "You could hear the special noise of the rocket and watch them fly or even glide for miles before coming down, causing much death and damage. I heard of fighter planes trying to shoot them down over the Channel, or tipping their wings to divert them away so they couldn't reach their targets. Throughout the orchards and vineyards the military set up small units consisting of a large truck from which a steel cable stretched up into the air holding a large fish-shaped silver balloon, hoping the bombs would be caught and crash down. Unfortunately, some did, right on the crew below!"

The Canadians had a camp on a hill near where the Jarvis' lived. They had large anti-aircraft guns set up and no locals were allowed near. When bombs fell in the area, they were always there along with the Americans from their nearby camps and were a great help to the local service people.

While in college, Una often worried whether her mother and her house would still be there when she returned each day. "It was a constant, deep down fear for me, especially because Hitler's V-2 rockets were launched in September."

She also recollects, "There was fear of the Germans invading England but as that great man, Mr. Churchill, said, "We will fight them on the beaches", etc. His indomitable spirit was indeed of a constant encouragement which kept people going through that great turmoil of war. During the war it was quite difficult, with fear filling every moment."

Una finished college in 1945. In March she and Connie got positions as secretaries in London with The Soft Drink Industry (War Time) Association Ltd. The company was formed by the government because sugar, being the main ingredient, was severely rationed. They travelled to London by train.

While working in London they met some young Canadian soldiers. As her brother, Lester, was in Canada, Una invited them to visit her home when they were on leave. Her parents wanted to respond with Canadian hospitality. The first one, Una reminiscences, "His name was Sammy Clark from northern Ontario and he was very tall. One day my mother went downtown, about a twenty minute walk away, to do some shopping and took him with her. It was quite a sight to see my mother, who was not even five feet tall, with Sammy walking by her side carrying her things home. He loved it. He was transferred to another place in England but his younger brother, Richard, started coming to our home with his pal, Bob Schenk from Saskatchewan."

Her cousin, Ken Huntington, from Toronto was in the Royal Canadian Air Force. While stationed in England, he too visited the Jarvis's on leave. With Connie and Una on their own bikes and, Ken on one of Una's brother's bikes, they peddled around the lovely Kentish countryside. Ken told them, "When the war is over come to Canada and visit."

Una did just that. After saving her money for three years, she and Connie along with another friend, Frieda bought a ship's passage. Arriving in Halifax their first venture was to the Eaton's store where they were thrilled to be able to buy nylon stockings. A luxury! After a long train ride, they arrived in Toronto. They worked there for a year before returning to England. Freida remained. Taking a train to New York and seeing all the sights they then sailed home on the Queen Mary liner.

She continued to live at home and worked in London for The Brush ABOE Group. After doing some traveling she decided she would like to return to Canada. In October, 1951 she booked a passage that would sail from Liverpool in June, 1952.

In the meantime she met Anthony Barrett, who worked for Tilton Sons and Co. a shipping company. He didn't think that he had much of a future in his position, so he asked Una to marry him and thus start a new life in Canada.

After marrying in June they set sail on the Ascania. On the ship Tony had been assigned a cabin with two little old ladies and Una a different cabin with a man with two little boys. They went to the Purser and he arranged another room for them so they could be together! Arriving in Montreal friends met them and drove them to Toronto. They lived in several cities before settling in Calgary. They have two daughters and a son.

Of the war Una said, "In the 1970's, I remember waking up thinking there was an air raid on, but of course, it was a storm – *quite a flashback to war time memories.*"

More than seventy years later Una and Connie remain close friends.

# CHAPTER THREE

## The Jarvis Brothers Sign Up

In England, brothers Lester and Alan Jarvis had been in the Air Cadets. It was natural then for both of them to want to be in the air force when the war began. However, to join any of the services you were supposed to be eighteen years old.

In those days students left school at fourteen and as Lester was expected to take responsibility with the family finances, he did so. He worked nights at a paper factory. The pulp for the paper came from Canada but, as the war progressed, little was shipped because of the high toll of German U-boats sinking Allied ships in the Atlantic.

Finally reaching eighteen in 1943, Lester signed up with the Royal Air Force. In October of that year he was sent by ship to Canada to train as a pilot under the British Commonwealth Air Training Plan. He landed in St. John, New Brunswick at first and did the majority of his training in Saskatchewan and just south of Vancouver. By the time he was finished, fighter pilots were not in great demand so he started training for air crew. There had been a possibility air crew would be needed in India on the 'rice run' for the Pacific hostilities in the summer of 1945, but the Japanese surrendered and there was no more war.

Alan finished two years at Dartford Technical School when he was sixteen. For a year afterwards he worked in a local butcher shop that was managed by a close neighbour. His special hobby was making model planes from balsa wood. He was also very interested in animals and birds, and had an aviary attached to the garden shed where he kept at least nine budgerigars.

Because of rationing each person in his family was only entitled to four ounces of meat, lamb and beef, per week. To supplement this he kept rabbits and chickens. When the chicks hatched his mother, Ethel, fed up the cockerels and for Christmas they had a good sized chicken to eat. Also as eggs were not available at the stores but replaced with egg powder from the U.S., his family was able to have fresh eggs from the chickens.

Now seventeen, at the end of 1943, Alan enlisted in the Royal Air Force. He trained in England to be part of an air crew. From December 31st he attended No 4 radio school for nine months on a long and extensive course as a wireless operator, 'a signaller'. When this was finished he transferred on October 6, 1944 to No 35 Operational Training Unit in Vickers Wellingtons.

He was assigned to Heavy Conversion Unit 1656, February 11, 1945 and started his bomber training, flying mainly with Flight Sergeant Roland Thorpe. His overseas flying began March 13th over eastern Germany on bombing runs in Avro Lancasters. With Thorpe as pilot they bombed the submarine yards at Hamburg on March 31st and on April 3rd bombed Nordhausen.

On the night of April 9th Alan's bomber was part of a thousand bomber raid - five hundred going over northern Germany and five hundred going in the southern direction. From their base at RAF Hemswell they took off at 19:32 hours. Along with Alan (Wireless Operator/Air Gunner: Sergeant) the crew consisted of Pilot: Flight Sergeant Roland Thorpe, Flight Engineer: Flight Sergeant Harry Blakey, Navigator: Flying Officer John Wotherspoon, Air Bombardier: Sergeant Frederick Goodenough, Air Gunner: Sergeant Richard Harford and Air Gunner: Sergeant Lawrence Hill.

Their mission that night was to attack the Deutsche Werke U-boat yard at Kiel, Germany. Kiel, 90 kilometres north of Hamburg, was a large German naval port for U-boats, warships and a shipbuilding centre producing submarines. On route they found out that the German battleship, the Admiral Scheer, had taken harbour there.

Unfortunately for Alan and his crew, the last communication heard from them was that they were going in for their bombing run. It is presumed that Alan's plane was so badly damaged that they were unable to send out a message and their plane went into the Baltic Sea. All the crew perished. On April 15th Alan would have been twenty years old.

Three aircraft were lost that night with only one crew member surviving. The RAF was notified as to where two of the planes had crashed. Alan's plane though was listed as lost without a trace.

On the morning of Alan's last flight his one canary, which was kept in a cage in the house, was found dead. It was a horrific omen and very painful for Ethel.

His sister, Una describes hearing the news of what had happened to her brother, "I came home from work and my father was sitting in his armchair crying and I said to my mother, "What is wrong with Dad?". My mother handed me the telegram that they had received from the Air Ministry, which stated that Alan was missing in action.

The wife of one of the engineers for whom she worked at The Soft Drink Industry (War Time) Association Ltd., was with the Air Ministry. She asked him, "Could you get me more information about Alan's plane going missing?" The next day he advised her, "The Admiral Scheer battleship was sunk at Kiel and three planes went down last night." This was later confirmed to the family.

Una remembered Sergeant Lawrence Hill, the rear gunner spending his last leave with Alan at their home around Christmas 1944. She and her parents later met the wife of the Navigator, John Wotherspoon, at the Northumberland Hotel, near Marble Arch in London. He was the only married crew member and had two children.

Una said, "During the war our greatest horror was losing Alan."

After the war Lester returned to England in 1946. He worked in London in the Ministry of Defence. He married and had two children. In his early 30's he contracted polio which left his right arm paralyzed.

Once recovered, he moved to a small village near his new government job and had a house built. Remembering his days in Canada and the homes having central heating, he built one like them. His parents later went to live with him.

Alan Jarvis in Royal Air Force uniform - WWII

Tuesday, 27th March, 1945

Dear Folks at Home,

One of these days or nights, it may be that I do not return from operations on which I am now engaged. I have no idea if this will happen but there is always a possibility that it will. I have no feeling (I believe you call it a premonition) of death, I am only just writing this in case it should happen and will leave it in a safe place.

I have no regrets, nor must you have any, only a deep pride in the knowledge that one of your sons has died for his country. I give it cheerfully because I believe that one day the world will be free from tyranny and the other horrors of war.

We must all make sacrifices at some time or other, I have made mine cheerfully and wish you to make yours as cheerfully as me, although I know yours is a greater sacrifice.

I feel great satisfaction to know some little boy or girl may someday learn that the sky is something beautiful and not just a huge bomb bay of fire and death. Also, some young mother may not fear the coming of night and young men can look forward to rearing the family in a far better world.

I do not know if I am afraid of death but it comes swiftly and I will not feel it.

I could not have wished for a better or happier time than I have had, or could have wished for more than I have had. I owe such a lot to you all and, by dying in this manner, I know that I have repaid just a little to you all. Knowing this in my heart, I die happy and content.

Goodbye until we meet again. God bless you all.

Alan

Alan Jarvis wrote this letter to his family.

# CHAPTER FOUR

## Forced Labour

J osef and Anna Skawinski had lived in the village of Gwozdziec, Poland with their daughter Stefka. For a time they lived in the United States where three sons, Stanislav, Larry and Jan were born. Upon their return Anna gave birth to sons, Stefan, Mijo and Boleslaw. With Anna's passing Josef remarried and had another son, Bronek.

Gwodzeic was located in the south, sixty kilometers east of Krakow.

Josef was a farmer. He had a large farm that produced grain and vegetables. Everyone helped out. The children were able to walk to a nearby school. There they were taught to speak Russian. Although the family did not have a lot they were very happy.

Poland was invaded by Germany on September 1, 1939 and the Soviet Union on September 17. In early October the two countries divided and annexed Poland, Germany to the west and the Soviet Union to the east. Complete occupation by Germany would take place after the summer of 1941.

The Nazis arrived in Gwodzeic in 1940. Everything in the village was taken, even the bell from the church for the metal. Joseph's farm was seized and the family was forced to leave and live elsewhere. At the time Boleslaw was fifteen years old.

During the war brothers Stanislav, Larry and Jan, lived in the United States. Boleslaw and Stefan remained in Poland. Things changed for them in 1943 when the Germans took them to Germany as unpaid forced labourers.

Boleslaw was forced to work on a farm forty kilometres north of Hanover. His brother Stefan was taken elsewhere. Boleslaw said, "I was not given much food to eat. It was basically bread and water. I was awakened at 4:00am and had to work very hard. In the winter I cut trees. It was a very sad time as I was separated from my family." He was kept there for the duration of the war.

Upon the war's end in May, 1945 the Skawinski farm reverted back to the family. However, Stefan and Boleslaw did not return to Poland.

Stefan remained in Germany. There he met his wife Mary Louise and their son was born. In 1949 they immigrated to Australia.

Boleslaw also stayed in Germany and went to Frankfurt. He was recruited by the American army, as part of a Polish regiment of three hundred men. Issued with a black U.S. uniform he wore it proudly. They sent him to Mannheim to be trained. At first he guarded American bombs.

Later he served as a guard on trains transporting SS men from Ludfexsburg to Dachau concentration camp where they were being held as prisoners awaiting trial for war crimes. There were two guards with machine guns on every second train car. If the guards saw a prisoner throw a note to their family out the window, they were to fire off a shot into the air. The train would then be stopped and backtracked to look for the note. Once found the train would continue. He was also ordered to shoot if anyone tried to escape. Asked if he had ever shot anyone he replied, "No." At Dachau he witnessed SS men being hung on a big tree outside the camp.

He served around eight months, until the fall of 1947, when he was discharged. The Polish army had been discontinued.

Boleslaw then went to a Displaced Person camp for Polish people in Heilbronn. Journeying to Stuttgart he obtained his medical so he could go to Canada on a three year mining contract. He left August, 1948 on the American army ship, the S.S. Swallow.

Landing in Halifax he travelled by train to Kirkland Lake and began his career as a hard rock miner. He remained there for the rest of his life. Until his death he was paid a small amount of compensation money from the Germans.

# CHAPTER FIVE

## Taken to Germany

Antoni and Jozefa Myszka lived in the city of Minsk, Belorussia.
In the early years Polish people migrated to Minsk and a Polish community was established with its language and culture dominating. Later when annexed by the Russian Empire, Russian was spoken. Apart from a few brief times between 1919 and 1921, when it was controlled by the Second Polish Republic, it was the capital of the Belorussian Soviet Socialist Republic within the Soviet Union. The Belarusian language was used in the 1920's and early 30's but reverted back to Russian in the late 30's.

Minsk was an important junction. The railway and a road ran through it which linked Moscow and Warsaw. The edges of the city were surrounded by forests.

Antoni and Jozefa considered themselves Polish and not Russian and spoke Polish at home. They had seven children: Janina, Jan, Josef, Kazik, Jadwiga and Eddek(Eddy). A seventh baby died of starvation. The children all learned Russian at school. They were a very close knit family and had many friends.

Eddy remembers this about his family, "Poland was under Russian occupation, and in 1912 they put our whole family onto cattle trains and shipped us out of Poland and off to Russia. My mother, Jozefa, was only six years old at the time."

Antoni was a farmer and Russians soldiers often pillaged his farm. When they entered his house, Jozefa had to cook for them. During this time Janina died. While going down to the cellar to get food she fell down the stairs. Injured internally they took her on a horse drawn cart to a doctor who said there was nothing he could do for her.

Of his father Eddy recalls, "In 1937 my father was arrested by the KGB, along with many other Polish men. He was taken to an island near the North Pole called, Novaya Zemlya, for hard labour. It was a place of no return."

The Germans began their invasion of the Soviet Union on June 22nd, 1941. At the end of the month they occupied Minsk. It became the administrative centre of Reichskomissariatn Ostland. Homes were requisitioned to house the conquering forces. Thousands of people starved as food was seized by the army and paid work was scarce.

As the city was being destroyed, Jadwiga remembers the bombs falling and that they had to go underground into shelters. She said, "One time I saw one of the guards who was guarding the shelter have his head blown off by a bomb. Another time one of my older brothers decided not to go to the shelter. He said, "Nothing is going to happen." This time our apartment building was hit but he was okay."

Jozefa, realizing that it was not safe to stay in the city, fled into the forest with her children. They took everything that they could carry with them. Jadwiga said, "As we were going through the forest we knew that if we were caught we would be killed. We would have been shot immediately. We had to take the chance though as we had no other choice."

They headed west as they did not want to go east to Russia. They were scared of running into the Russians as they did not like them. Since they had already taken Antoni away, Jozefa was fearful they would also take her sons.

When they encountered some German soldiers Jozefa told them that she wanted to return to Poland. They agreed to this and put the whole family on a train. However, the train didn't stop in Poland but went straight through the country to Germany.

When they arrived they were sent to work at a labour camp which was under guard. Of the war time Eddy says, "I don't remember very much as I was only nine when the war ended but I know that my family was treated very badly, first by the Russians and later in Germany."

With the war over, they were free, but could not return to Poland or Russia. They went to a Displaced Persons camp in Heilbronn. Through the Red Cross they found out that Antoni had died in Novaya Zemlya in 1942.

After what the family had experienced this camp was like heaven to them. They were fed and had a place to sleep. With a love for singing Jadwiga joined the choir. She made many new friends including a special one named Boleslaw Skawinski.

At that time there were only three countries that would accept displaced persons: Canada, the United States and Australia. Jozefa was a single woman with four sons so only Australia would give her entry. Eddy said, "We waited a few years, then took a chance and left for Melbourne in 1950."

Jadwiga was able to get a contract as a domestic in Canada. She departed Hamburg in December, 1948 on the MS Sobieski, a Polish passenger ship. Arriving in Halifax she took a train to Port Hope, Ontario where she was to work. Within a few months she was unhappy. She shared this with Boleslaw with whom she was still romantically involved. He bought out her contract, brought her to Kirkland Lake and married her.

It was there that they raised their family. As they learned English and their children brought it home from school it gradually became the only language spoken. Boleslaw said, "We are in a new country now and English is the language here." Polish customs were still kept as that was all that they knew.

Their daughter Helen recalls, "My mother spoke a lot about what she had experienced during the war so that I would understand. My father never spoke of it until in 2009 when I went to Poland to see where he was born, meet the family that was there and to visit the graves of my grandparents as I wanted to know my history. After I returned he talked freely about what he had gone through."

Jozefa Myszka and her children.

1949 - Wedding of Jadwiga and Boleslaw Skawinski.

# CHAPTER SIX

## A Mother's Determination to save her Children

Rachelle and Wolf Ber Mydlarski lived a simple but happy life in Paris, France. They had five children: Jacques, Henri, Dora, Micheline and Robert. They owned a small retail business.

France declared war on Germany in September, 1939. By May, 1940 Germany launched an invasion into the country. Wolf Ber, called to serve in the French army, was sent to the front lines to fight the invaders.

Many Parisians, fearing the German advancement left Paris. They travelled westward on the highways. Some transported their belongings in push carts. Rachelle fled with her children. Jacques, her eldest was eight years old. Having a large family allowed her to be able to travel by bus. They frequently had to jump off and lie down in the ditches to protect themselves from gunfire that came from German airplanes. Countless people died.

Arriving in Bois-Joli, Brittany, they were taken in by a farmer named Pere Henri. The little village was occupied by the Germans. An officer, who spoke some French, asked all the villagers to gather together in the town's square. He spoke to them and said, "People, do not fear us Germans, we, like you, are civilized. We do not want to harm you. We just want to get rid of the blacks, the Gypsies, the homosexuals and the Jews." After a short stay there, they returned home.

In June, France surrendered to Germany and Italy. They signed an armistice at Compiègne. The country was divided into an occupied northern zone and an unoccupied southern zone. Paris, which had fallen on the 14th, was now in the occupied zone and under direct German control.

On September 21, Jewish people were forced to go to their regional police station to register and receive identity cards. The cards bore the inscription 'Jew' and were affixed with a red seal. Their names, addresses, profession and nationality were written on filing cards and kept by the French police who later handed the cards over to the Gestapo.

Many more rules applied to Jewish people. Jacques sums up some of them, "Jews were not allowed to possess a radio, nor go to the movies, and we had to ride in the last wagon of the trains, or in the back of the bus. We also had a curfew and had to be off the streets by 8:00pm."

The Germans demanded that the French provide food for their troops and food to be sent to Germany. In response to this request the government had to ration milk, bread, meat, cheese, sugar, butter, margarine and rice. For Jewish people it was even harder. Jacques explains, "It was extremely difficult for my mother to have enough food to feed us as Jews were forbidden to go shopping for food before 11:00am. There was a shortage of everything in France, so, when 11 o'clock came, everything had been sold, and the shelves in the stores were completely empty."

Wolf Ber had been able to return home from the battle field unhurt but his luck did not last. When the Nazis rounded up the heads of Jewish families in May of 1941 he was arrested and sent to Beaune-la-Rolande transit camp, where he was interned. His family received a letter from him saying that he and other prisoners were being sent to an unknown destination.

Rachelle and her children lived in a five story apartment building located near the Renault factory in Boulogne-Billancourt. The factory manufactured armaments for the German army. The allies, aware of this fact, tried to destroy the factory by bombing it in March of 1942. Their home was hit and destroyed. They lost everything but had survived by taking shelter in the basement of the building. To get out, they had to dig themselves out of the rubble and walk over corpses. Because of her large family, Rachelle was able to find another apartment and moved to a different area.

At the end of May, 1942 Jewish people over the age of six were required to wear the yellow badge. Rachelle and her children were summoned to present themselves at the police station, to receive their yellow stars, with the printed word 'JUIF' on it. The stars then had to be sewn on the left side of their outer garments.

On July 16 and 17 foreign Jews living in Paris from Germany, Austria, Poland, Czechoslovakia, the Soviet Union and those who were stateless, were rounded up by the police. They were taken to Vélodrome d'Hiver sports arena. There they were packed in without food, water or sanitary facilities. After five days, they were taken to Drancy, Pithiviers, and Beaune-la-Rolande camps and then deported by train to Auschwitz. The majority perished including Rachelle's sister Paulette and her family.

Realizing that soon they would be coming for French Jews, Rachelle went to a nearby convent, to implore the Mother Superior, to please save her children, not asking anything for herself. The Mother Superior said, "The convent is only for nuns and they could not take in any children." Seeing Rachelle in tears, she took pity on her and gave her the name and address of Father Theomir Devaux, a priest at the Church of Notre-Dame of Zion.

Father Devaux, a saintly man, endeavoured to find Christian homes, willing to take in and shelter Jewish children, at the peril of their own lives. He was suspected by the Gestapo and was under constant surveillance. His office was regularly inspected. He agreed to help Rachelle and placed all her children in different locations with families throughout France.

Jacques and his brother Henri were given new false identification documents with the assumed family name of Boyer. They were sent to the village of Conches in Normandy. There they lived on a large estate run by two elderly ladies, Mme. Auclair and Mlle. Vandenberg, who were sworn to keep their secret. The property was owned by a Parisian industrialist, Mr.Tailleur, whom they had never met.

The estate, having been requisitioned by the German army, was used as a military camp. Many Nazi soldiers were stationed there. They were unaware that the two boys living with them were in fact, two Jewish boys in hiding. The estate was surrounded by an airport, a main railroad station and a depot of gasoline, hidden in the forest. The allies knew this and bombed the area constantly. Often Jacques and Henri had to spend the night in the cellar, to protect themselves from the bombs.

There was also a little house on the estate where they spent most of their time in the winter, as it was the only place that was heated. One evening, the ladies with whom they lived with wanted to sleep in the little house, but Jacques and Henri preferred to sleep in the estate. There they had their own room with separate beds, next to rooms occupied by the German soldiers. Everyone then decided to sleep in the estate. That night, another air raid by the allies happened and the little house received a direct hit and was completely destroyed. Jacques said, "Again G-d was watching over us."

Rachelle was also able to hide. She was taken in by friends who lived in a small apartment in Paris. When visitors came, she hid in a tiny kitchen cabinet.

France's liberation began in June and ended in December of 1944. During this time Paris was liberated in August.

Rachelle and all her children survived. At the end of the war, Jacques and Henri found out where their siblings had been hidden.

Sadly, after being taken to Beaune-la-Rolande camp, Wolf Ber was transported in a cattle train to Auschwitz concentration camp where he was murdered.

Father Devaux managed to save more than 500 Jewish children. He passed away after a long illness in January, 1967 at the age of 82. On September 5th, 1996, the title, "Righteous among the Nations", was accorded to him by the State of Israel, and was inscribed on the wall of honour in Yad Vashem. On March 25th, 1997 at a ceremony in Paris, he was honoured posthumously with a certificate and medal with the inscription from Hebrew: "Who Saves One Life Saves the Whole World." Present were church dignitaries, Jewish civil and political representatives, and some of the children he had helped to hide and save.

Jacques now resides in Calgary, Alberta.

# CHAPTER SEVEN

## Germans in the House

Despite the Netherlands declaration of neutrality in the beginning of September, 1939, Germany invaded the country on May 10th, 1940. When Rotterdam was bombed on the 14th many people died, countless homes were destroyed and the Dutch capitulated the following day.

With the surrender imminent, the government and royal family escaped and went into exile in London. There they formed a government-in-exile. Upon their refusal to return a German civilian government was set up, the Reichskommissariat Niederlande.

At this time Lamberdina and Willem Lindeboom had been married for three years. They lived in Wezep, a small village, about one hundred and three kilometres north east of Amsterdam. All the villagers were friendly with each other.

They lived in a very big two story house with their infant son, Frank. Like most of the community, they were a middle class family and had a good life. Willem worked as a bricklayer.

As the war began a railway near their home was bombed. Two military barracks that were located there stored ammunition and other goods. The Germans did not want the Dutch to have any supplies to use against them.

Blackout rules were applied. Not wanting British pilots, who flew over the Netherlands at night on route to bomb targets in Germany and navigated by looking down to know where they were, windows had to be covered up so no light shone through. Outside, matches and flashlights were also prohibited from being used.

On June 18 anything made from copper, lead, tin and nickel had to be handed in so they could be recycled and used for weapons production. The Dutch resisted and hid or buried their possessions in the ground to keep the Germans from getting them. Later in the war when orders were given for all radios to be turned in, Lamberdina said, "We hid ours under the floor in the living room."

Dutch money called guilders was made of silver. This was something else people were not supposed to possess. Consequently Lamberdina recalled, "We turned ours into bracelets and spoons just like everyone else did."

Rationing came into effect. The Lindebooms registered and received their ration cards. With them they were able to obtain coupons from one of the distribution offices that were staffed by the Dutch. The number of stamps one received depended on the size and ages of the family. The coupons were then used to purchase coffee, tea, bread, flour, meat, milk, potatoes, clothes, shoes, natural gas and electricity.

However, even with ration stamps there was a limited amount of food one could acquire. At the outset of the war Dutch warehouses had a sizeable stockpile but as the war progressed the Germans commandeered it and shipped it to Germany to feed their own people.

By October the Lindebooms were given ID cards with their pictures on it. Everyone over the age of fifteen had to have one.

Arbeitseinsatz was imposed on Dutch men. Those between the ages of eighteen and forty-five were forced into mandatory labour and sent to work in factories in Germany.

Willem said, "I didn't want to go. My only alternative was to hide." The decision was a difficult one for him to make as individuals had to hand in their ration cards and if he hid he wouldn't be able to get food. He would have to acquire a fake or stolen card. In spite of this he decided to hide anyway.

Along with a neighbour, the two of them hid in his home at night so the Germans would not discover them when they came to search the house in the evenings. A secret compartment was made at the back of a closet in the attic with a false wall. The compartment was very small and there was only enough room for them to sit in it. Willem recalled, "Even with this effort I was found and forcibly taken to a labour camp in Oberndorf, Germany, close to the Austrian border."

The factories at Oberndorf, a major centre of the German weapons industry, were quite often bombed by the allies. Willem was put to work making ammunition for which he received no compensation. It was free labour. Conditions in the large factory where he worked were far from pleasant. The food they were given to eat was lousy. The only communication he had with Lamberdina was when the Germans occasionally permitted someone to go home for a week and he could give letters to that person to give to her. Many Dutch people who worked there were very sad and they all wanted to go home.

He was supposed to remain at Oberndorf for two years. However, after one year, he was given a pass to return home for a short time. Upon being with Lamberdina he decided not to go back. Knowing it meant he had to go into hiding once again, he headed to the south of Holland where he was hidden by a family.

Even though it was a risk, every now and then he went back to see Lamberdina. After one such visit he decided to stay for good so he could be close to everyone.

He had to hide in different places every night in his neighbourhood. Sometimes he slept under the twigs that were used to make baskets and were left to dry in big piles beside homes. At other times he hid with people in fields and different places. Several women in the village and his wife always found a way to make sure that those in hiding had something to eat.

Willem said, "Even though I had to hide, I was glad to be home so that I could be near my family. I felt that it was better than life in Germany."

Gleichschaltung was implemented by the Germans. Everyone had to conform. Non-Nazi organizations were abolished. Socialist and Communist parties were forbidden. Only the the Nationaal-Socialistische Beweging political party was accepted. These Dutch collaborators or NSB-ers as they were called worked with the Germans and were part of the lower government and civil service. They received a price for turning in Jewish people. It was Dutch turning in the Dutch and they were hated.

There was a lot of caution going on in Wezep. People had to be very careful with what they said and did. Villagers had been taken to the forest and shot if the Germans knew they were against them. Willem said, "I witnessed people that I knew being shot in the head on a hill in the woods near my home."

With Willem in hiding and unable to work there was a lack of finances coming in for Lamberdina. She therefore had to become a resourceful woman, especially since the family had grown to include their daughter, Aaltje.

Not relying exclusively on her ration coupons she grew vegetables and sewed the family's clothes. When occasionally a parachute was found, she recycled the material and turned it into outfits. For fuel in the winter she used wood that came from the trees nearby and coal.

Despite the curfew that was enforced to restrict people's movements and not allow them to be out after dark, Lamberdina's brother, Jan, came from time to time, in the middle of the night, to bring her food. Frank remembers, "One night, while bringing meat, Uncle Jan was almost caught by the Germans. He had to sneak through the woods as they were after him, but he made it to our house. After that, Uncle Jan was really scared. Had he been caught he would have been shot."

Willem's sister, Geertje, also helped when she could. She worked on a farm and was therefore able to obtain food which she shared with Lamberdina.

Although she was unable to acquire things like sugar, soap or nylons, her family never went hungry. But food in the large cities like Amsterdam became scarce as there was little left in the stores. A lot of people walked for days and days to the countryside in search of food and were very hungry. Many times, after cooking a meal for her family and folks arrived, she gave them her own food to eat.

Unwelcome, the Germans began sleeping in the homes in Wezep. Home owners had no choice in this matter and were not compensated. Lamberdina and her children were restricted to the first floor of their house which had a bedroom, living room and a place to cook food. The second floor was off limits to them. There about ten soldiers slept on straw and, as they had lice, it went into the straw.

Frank recalls, "During the daytime, when the soldiers were out, I was curious and often snuck upstairs and went into the room where they slept to see what was there. One of the things that I saw were big jars of Dutch silver money. My mother would get very mad at me for going there." She would scold me, "Don't go upstairs again." "Of course, being a boy, I went up whenever I had a chance to look around."

Towards the end of the war, when Lamberdina was pregnant with Evertje, her third child, a very young German soldier said to her, "My wife is pregnant too and I feel very sorry for you. I am sorry I am in the war. I was forced to be a soldier and I do not want to be here." After the baby's birth, he brought her milk. Once in a while, the soldiers gave her some of the food that they had. She accepted it for it was a matter of life or death as she had to feed her family.

Although most of the soldiers were nice to her as they did not want to be there, she never trusted them. In fact she didn't trust anyone. Lamberdina remarked, "On the surface I was civil but I was extremely careful what I said to them as I was afraid they might shoot me. I was uncomfortable with them being in my home and never befriended them."

In September 1944, the southern part of the Netherlands was liberated. Finally on May 5, 1945 when the Germans surrendered the remainder of the country was freed.

Wezep was liberated by the Canadians.

With the help of the people in his village whom he trusted, Willem had been able to hide for a year until the war ended. He had many close calls, but was never found.

Lamberdina recalls, "The years during the war were very scary. When the sirens went off, I was afraid. There was no place to hide when the planes dropped their bombs. We did have a cellar under the house but it was just a small room. It had concrete walls containing shelves used to store vegetables and at least I could go down the stairs to this place to hide."

Lamberdina and Willem said, "There was joy and relief that the war was finally over. At last we could be together as a family."

The war years had been very difficult for both of them but they strove to put their life back together again and it gradually returned to normal. Lamberdina remarked, "My house took weeks to clean though as it was hard to get rid of the lice from when the soldiers were there." Various things, especially luxuries, could not be obtained as there were still shortages. Willem was able to return to his job as a bricklayer as there was no scarcity of work for him. The country needed to be rebuilt.

Their daughter, Evertje, recalls that her parents were open in talking about the war. What her mother experienced though affected her and she thinks that subconsciously she picked up on her mother's fears. "As a child I was always very scared if my mother went away or if she was just out of the house in the yard. When I knew she was gone I was always very scared for her. I never felt this way about my father." She always felt a need to protect them especially as they got older because of what they had endured. She never wanted them to be hurt as she sensed that they had been through enough.

She had a good childhood and is close to her younger brother, Henk, who was born after the war. She said, "My parents instilled in me to be honest, nice, and speak my mind."

Evertje and her husband and daughter immigrated to Calgary, Alberta in 1969. Holland was very densely populated and Canada had open spaces. Calgary in particular was close to the mountains which they loved. They flew by plane to Montreal, took a train to Edmonton and then finished their journey on a bus to Calgary. They knew life would be better for them in Canada.

1937 – Wedding of Lamberdina and Willem Lindeboom.

Dutch silver coins made into spoons during WWII.

# CHAPTER EIGHT

## Sisters in Holland

H endrika and Thomas de Waal married in 1923 in Watergang, Netherlands. They lived in the small village of Landsmeer, which was located about four kilometers north of Amsterdam. Their first child, Dirk was born the following year. Over time they would have thirteen more children: Johanna, Bep, Albert, Alie, Sandy, Mien, Tom, Margre, Hendrika, Henry, Jack, Bill and John.

Thomas worked in a warehouse sorting and packing eggs, which were then exported to England. Hendrika stayed home and took care of the house and family. They paid twenty five cents for each child to attend a private school.

Their one story house was located in the centre of the village. It had a kitchen, dining room, living room and a bedroom for Thomas and Hendrika, which always had a crib in it. A large attic was where the children slept. It was divided by a chimney and the girls were on one side and the boys on the other. Margre, remembers, "There were three in a bed."

Flowers decorated the lawn in front of their home. Behind their house were four acres of grassland with a barn on it for keeping their six dairy cows and a pig. There was also an apple and a pear tree along with fruit bushes and a big vegetable garden. Their washing machine and a cistern for keeping milk cool were kept there. As they had no indoor plumbing an outdoor stove heated the water that they used to take a bath. It was then brought inside and put in a galvanized tub. Hendrika joked, "Bathing started with the youngest one and then went up the line. You didn't want to be the last one."

An outhouse was built over a ditch that surrounded their home on three sides. The ditch was five feet wide and had retaining walls. It wound its way throughout the village and as there was no sewer system it contained waste water and rain from the fields. To cross over the ditch that was in front of their home, to get to the road, they used a little bridge.

At the beginning of May, 1940 Margre started school. "I was on the bridge and I saw a Dutch soldier in uniform with a rifle. Four days later the war started."

Standing in front of her house among the flowers, Margre remembers being scared of the arrival of the German soldiers. "I heard the sound of their boots on the cobblestones and voices singing. I was intimidated by them because one had no say in anything". They had a lookout at the top of one of the church steeples, which had a walk around. From there they kept watch over the whole village and the sky for airplanes.

The de Waals considered themselves not as bad off as some because of where they lived. In nearby Amsterdam an airplane factory was located on the north side of the city. The Germans tried to bomb it. Hendrika recalls, "We could always hear the bombings, the Germans at first and then the Allies. The single pane of our windows would rattle when the bombs fell and as we lay in bed we tried to cover our ears from all the sounds."

Throughout her life Margre said, "I never forget the sound of the air raid sirens." In her later years she experienced hearing a siren and her immediate thoughts were that the Germans were coming.

Due to his age and the fact that he had a large family, Thomas was not conscripted by the Germans. No longer able to work at the warehouse, as the export business was stopped and needing to support his family, he turned to selling wooden shoes to farmers and people in the village. He journeyed everywhere on a bicycle that had a metal basket on the front that could hold his merchandise.

In Amsterdam, Jewish people were taken away to concentration camps and their businesses confiscated. Although it was forbidden by the Germans to do commerce with them, Thomas and Hendrika did, despite the risk of getting caught and also transported. They purchased goods such as vacuum cleaners and textiles as they would sooner see the de Waals have things at cost then for the Germans to take them. Thomas then sold those items to further support his family.

Thomas and Hendrika were very sympathetic towards the Jewish people. They were friends with many and tried to help them whenever they could. She would always say, "Don't say anything against the Jew because they are the apple of God's eye."

Thomas worked with the Dutch underground. His job was to take Jewish people from one hiding place to another. It was dangerous work and if captured he would have been sent to a concentration camp. Margre remembers the school inspector being taken away.

To feed her family Hendrika canned the vegetables that she grew in her garden and in the fall a big hole was dug up in the earth to make a cold cellar. The top was dirt and straw and vegetables like cabbage were put in it to preserve them over the winter. She also made her own cheese.

Although young, Hendrika remembers people continuously coming to their house for food because of their proximity to the city. "My mother always had bean soup on the stove and whenever anybody came to the door mum gave them a bowl of soup. I don't remember ever being hungry."

Clothing a big family during the war was not easy. The children wore clothes passed down from one to another. Hendrika also had a seamstress who made things for them such as coats. Everyone wore knitted, homemade socks.

Every now and then the Germans came and checked their house to see if they had a radio, which was forbidden. They had hidden theirs under the floor boards in the hallway and even though they could not speak English they listened to the BBC. They also had a small, metal box with a key, which the children called the 'money box'. It was buried in a hole in the back yard with what little money that they had.

With no gas or electricity, as it had been cut off by the Germans, they used kerosene lamps and cookers (hotplates). They also had a stationary bicycle that they used to charge a battery that was hooked up to it to make light and for their radio to work. They heated their house with coal and peat.

One advantage of having so many children was that no Germans stayed in their home. Margre and Hendirka both recall though, that some soldiers stayed at the village orphanage.

During the war Margre and Hendrika went to school and tried to live life as normally as possible. They played and did all sorts of things. At the time, they did not know of their father's activities with the Dutch underground. Hendrika recalls, "The least we knew the safer we were as the Germans could ask us questions."

Even though she was a child, Margre remembers the NSB-ers. It was a known thing that they were women friendly with the German soldiers. "After the war they took those women on a hay cart, shaved their hair off, then tarred and feathered them. That kind of made me sick." Hendrika said, "There were men also. They were talked about that they could be NSB-ers. So we had to be careful of what we said around them."

In 1943, both Margre and Hendrika got tonsillitis from swimming in the contaminated water in the ditch. They were supposed to have their tonsils out but, as the doctor was a German, their mother would not allow it.

The Germans caught up with Dirk in the spring of 1944. Prior to this, he had managed to elude them, thanks to someone at the church he attended being on the lookout. During the service, if the Germans came up the long church walkway it would be announced and the young men would run away. This time he didn't make it and was sent to Germany to work on a farm as a farmhand.

After many months, an elderly German couple helped Dirk escape and he returned home. Arriving in the middle of the night he knocked on the door. Thomas asked, "Who is it?" As a joke, he replied, "It's the Gestapo. Open up." The family was so relieved and overjoyed to see it was him. So as not to be caught again, he went into hiding at his girlfriend's farm about eight kilometers away.

In October, some of the kids got hepatitis. Hendrika said, "If one person got something it easily spread to the others."

Then, in December, several of the children came down with typhoid. It started with Klaas, Johanna's boyfriend. He had been hiding with the de Waals to avoid being taken by the Germans and didn't know he had it. It came from the water and raw milk as the cows drank from the ditch. Hendrika recognized the symptoms as her siblings had had it during WWI. Dirk also contracted the typhoid and regrettably passed it on to his girlfriend's family so he had to return home. Fortunately, Margre and her sister Hendrika did not catch it.

Banners were posted all over the outside of their house and in the trees saying that their home was under quarantine. There was no medicine available to treat the children. Hendrika cared for them during the day and Thomas during the night. As their fevers were very high, a health nurse helped with bathing them in the mornings. With soap not readily available, Thomas went from house to house bartering for some, so the sickness would not spread.

The Germans were afraid of catching typhoid, so they didn't dare enter their place. This proved to be a blessing. As animals were not allowed to be slaughtered, another German order, farmers secretly brought theirs on a small barge, along the ditch, to the grassy area at the back of their house. There they were killed and the meat distributed.

Margre vividly remembers that Christmas. "I asked my older sister Johanna, who was a midwife, if she had gotten a Christmas tree." She replied, "There were none left so I bought an apple tree." I said, "That was no good." Johanna said, "Sneak downstairs and see what you think of it." "What I saw was a big tree that touched the ceiling and was decorated with real candles." Sadly that was Johanna's last Christmas as she succumbed to typhoid the following April.

She also recalls it being the winter when two Allied plane crew were killed by the Germans. Their plane had been shot down and crashed. Margre said, "The crew were caught and shot against a fence because they had hidden. I can still remember seeing their pictures in the newspaper."

At the end of 1944 the western provinces of Holland suffered a calculated famine by the Germans, known as the "Hunger Winter". They deprived the Dutch of food and fuel by way of cutting off provisions from the farming regions. Although emergency soup kitchens were set up, multitudes died of starvation. Both Margre and Hendrika remember seeing people collapsed on the streets of their village.

The de Waal's had enough food until March of 1945. Margre was then sent to the town kitchen to collect a pot of soup and a couple of loaves of bread for her family. In addition to the food, she also came home with lice, after standing in line next to people. Her long hair was cut into a short bob.

As Holland was not yet liberated, in May, the Allies dropped desperately needed food parcels by parachute from airplanes. The packages were taken to the town hall where the food was divided up and distributed according to the size of the family. Margre remembers, "I had my first stick of gum which I had never tasted before. There was also corn beef in a can, big cream crackers that were beautiful, and shepherd's pie in big tins." This continued throughout June and July.

The end of the war was filled with celebration. Dutch flags were brought out and flown. There was dancing in the streets. Their village had a parade with a band. Bicycles were decorated with crepe paper through the spokes of their wheels.

In Amsterdam their aunt though, was almost killed. Hendrika recalls, "With the arrival of the Canadians everyone went kind of crazy. She was among a throng of people at a square, when the Germans came out. Even though they knew they had lost the war they started shooting and everyone scattered. Fortunately, she was able to get away safely."

After the war employment was difficult to find. Thomas was able to get work at the airplane factory in north Amsterdam making Fokker airplanes. Hendrika continued to take care of her home and family.

Undernourished children from their village were sent to England as there was nothing in Holland. The stores were empty and there was still rationing for things like sugar and butter. Their cousin was one of the ones who went. Hendrika and Margre both said, "We wanted to go but we were too healthy."

Deciding to emigrate, the de Waals had a choice of going to Australia, Africa or Canada, as those places were open to Dutch immigrants. Canadian farmers needed farm workers and offered to sponsor them. The only requirement was for an agent to make sure there would be living quarters and a guaranteed season of work. With that in place, in May of 1952, Thomas and Hendrika and six sons, Sandy, Tom, Henry, Jack, Bill and John, along with daughters Margre and Hendrika left for Canada. Another son, Albert, and his family would join them a year later.

Sailing on the S.S. Sicbyak, they arrived nine days later in Halifax at Pier 21. Taking a train to Lethbridge, Alberta they were met at the station by a farmer with his big truck. They drove north to Picture Butte and began work on a sugar beet farm. Margre and Hendirka worked as hired girls in the house.

After the harvest, a field man who looked after immigrants, arranged for Thomas, Margre, and Tom to work at United Trailers in High River. In November, the rest of the family joined them. While at this job, Margre met Willis Graham, a widower with a young son.

Willis was from Manitoba and had signed up in 1939 to fight the war. As a tank operator with the Fort Garry Horse Armoured Regiment, he landed on D-Day at Normandy in 1944 and then continued fighting in Belgium. There he got diphtheria and was sent to England to get well. Recovered, he rejoined the combat at Arnhem,

Holland. After, he crossed the border into Germany and heading north, returned to Holland and fought in the battle at Groningen. From there, he went south to Apeldoorn, where he was billeted with a Dutch family. Returning to England, he was shipped back to Canada in 1946. Willis came home with an English war bride, Iris. Sadly, she and their newborn daughter drowned in a tragic, river ferry accident.

Margre and Willis married and relocated to Portage la Prairie, Manitoba. She loved Willis's son as her own and they had seven more sons.

Hendrika went to Calgary in 1955. She married Joe Pente and they raised two girls and two boys.

Joe, an emigrant from Hungary, was born in a small town on the Hungarian border. The town was nicknamed, 'Little Palestine', as many Jewish people lived there. He loved and respected them, and as a boy lit the fires for them on Friday nights and Saturdays. He remembers, "One day, during the war, the Germans came and took them and put them on a train."

When he was around twelve years old, the boys in his town were also told to get on a train. Instead of showing up at the station, he and a friend hid for twenty four hours. When they came out from hiding the mayor of the town told them to go play. Very few of the boys that left returned home as they had been sent to Germany and forced to join the Hitler Youth.

After the war, the borders changed and Joe's town was now part of Czechoslovakia. In 1950, he escaped to West Germany. While staying at a refugee camp, he was given the choice of going to Brazil or Canada. Choosing the latter, he arrived in 1951 and worked in the bush in northern Ontario before going to Calgary in 1954.

Thomas and Hendrika moved to Port Alberni, British Columbia in 1956. After seventeen years there they returned to Alberta.

Five years ago Margre and Hendrika found out that they are Jewish through their mother.

1943 - Hendrika, Alie, Mien and Margre de
Waal, Volendam, Netherlands

Willis Graham - WWII

1952 - The de Waal family gather in the backyard of
their home in Landsmeer, just before leaving for Canada.
Back row, third left Margre, second right Hendrika

# CHAPTER NINE

## Escape from France

I saac and Bertha Teitelbaum lived in Riga, Latvia with their thirteen children. They were a very close knit family. They lived in a Jewish community but were assimilated within Riga culture. They held an equal class as everyone else did.

Isaac, who was in the lumber business, had his own company. One son Moisjes, or Monia as everyone called him, worked with his father. Monia was very knowledgeable and had a good command of numerous languages. He spoke Yiddish at home, English, French, German, Russian, Finnish, Swedish, Spanish, Italian, Hungarian and a little Greek.

To promote his father's business Monia moved to Paris, France, when he was in his mid-twenties. He loved the city and thought it was a wonderful place to live. There he became best friends with Rudy Bloomberg and they enjoyed being a part of the social scene. They went to the best clubs and the finest hotels.

However, when the Nazis entered Paris in June, 1940 everything changed for him. With the country divided and Paris under German control, he thought it wise to escape. Although his family was in Latvia he made the decision to head south to Spain. To do this he had to slip into the unoccupied southern zone and travel through it. A collaborationist government had been set up there in the town of Vichy. It was dangerous to be in this zone as Vichy administrators and police turned over French and foreign Jews to the Gestapo.

Making it safely over the border into Spain he was jailed for a couple of days because he was there illegally. When released he fled again, this time over the mountains to Switzerland. Having been a body builder, he physically attached himself to the undercarriage of a train car that was going there. At one point he almost ended up back in France because the direction of the train changed. Upon arriving he got work as a pot washer in the kitchens. His best friend Rudy was with him as they had travelled together.

In July of 1941 Monia lost contact with his family when Latvia was occupied by the Germans. The country had become part of Germany's Reichskommissariat Ostland. He was concerned for them. His younger brother, Harry, at the age of 26 had only been practising medicine for a year or two.

Monia stayed in Switzerland until 1942 and then left Europe. He went to Palestine. He was not a Zionist, in fact he was not religious at all, but it was possibly the only place that would accept Jews at the time. He hung out in the restaurants and bars and met people like Moshe Dayan and Golda Meir as Palestine was not a very big a community.

Now married, he remained until 1948 when the marriage ended. Then he went to Helsinki, Finland, as he had been there before the war with his father on business trips.

When he arrived, with no money and only two nice business suits, he went to the nicest hotel in the entire city. He asked the man behind the desk, "Do you remember me? I came here a lot with my father."

The man replied, "Yes, I remember you."

Monia inquired, "I would like the nicest room in the entire hotel and I would like it for a month."

The man said, "I'm sorry it is not available for a month but we do have this other room which is quite nice and you can have it for a month."

Monia said, "That will not do, but I'll take it under the provision that you invoice me after one month and the invoice has to be categorically stated as such, and if it is not to my satisfaction I won't pay you until it is to my satisfaction."

The man responded, "Okay, Mr. Teitelbaum. That is fine."

What Monia basically bought with no money, was thirty days of credit, when it was quite difficult to be able to establish any. Over the next thirty days he worked very hard to generate enough revenue so he could actually pay his bill. He ended up living at the hotel for the next year.

Not long after his arrival he met Saga Nyberg who worked in the night club across the street from the hotel. She was the head hostess and was in charge of greeting guests as they came in. When he first met her he told her, "You are going to be my wife." She replied, "No I'm not going to be your wife as I'm already married and have a son. Marrying you isn't going to happen." He pursued her and frequented the club on a regular basis. Discovering that her husband had been unfaithful she relayed the story to Monia. His reply, "Great, now we can get married."

In 1953 Monia, Saga, and her son moved to Montreal where they married. They had a good life with an upper middle class home in Mount Royal. They had two children, both of whom were named after his siblings.

Monia was a very astute business man and had chosen Montreal as the city to set up his lumber business headquarters. From there he could travel to other parts of Canada to acquire the trees that Europe needed. He also chose it as Jews tended to go where other Jews were, and given a choice of there or Winnipeg he chose the former. He maintained a strong relationship with others that had escaped the war and escaped the concentration camps and survived.

His friend Rudy also lived in Montreal and became his business partner. Rudy had married Alice, who grew up as a child in Sweden. Alice's life had been spared by the diplomat Raoul Wallenberg. Her mother had survived the gas chambers three times. One time after being lined up to be shot and put in a ditch she hid under the bodies of the dead and pretending to have also died she was able to crawl out. Alice was fortunate to have her mother living with her in Montreal.

Immediately after the Germans had occupied Latvia, mass killings of Jewish people took place. By the end of 1941 almost all had been killed. This included Isaac and Bertha and twelve of their children. A single death record was found, that of Harry, the doctor. He had been sent to Estonia and died there in a concentration camp. Apart from Monia the only other family members to survive were an uncle and a first cousin that had moved to Johannesburg, South Africa in the 1930s.

Monia's son Harry recalls, "My parents did not talk much about the war." Saga who had been in Finland said, "It was a tough life. Subsistence living." "My father didn't experience what a lot of other Jews experienced by being in a concentration camp. He was never really captured so he didn't have that horrific sense. Of course he lost all his siblings and that is dreadful enough in itself but he wasn't physically there. He considered himself fortunate. He was sad with the loss of his family but he never grieved as far as I could tell."

Moisjes Teitelbaum, front row, far left, with his
parents and siblings in Latvia, mid 1930's.

# CHAPTER TEN

## Jewish in Egypt

Aref and Bahaya Bochi were born in Syria. At that time Damascus was governed by the French so they had French nationality. In need of a safe place to live they moved to Cairo, Egypt. Three daughters, Olga, Marcel, another daughter and three sons, Sami, Fredi and Charles were born there. Children were given the nationality of their parents if they were not Arab, so they were considered French.

Egypt had become a de facto British colony in 1882 and was granted its independence in 1922. However Britain continued to influence the country politically and their troops remained around the Suez Canal zone.

The Bochi's lived in a fairly large and close knit Jewish community. Although Aref was quite a religious man he didn't force his beliefs on others.

The family were reasonably well off. Aref owned a cigar store but made his money by doing black market money exchanging behind his building. He called himself 'a banker'.

When the Italians invaded Egypt in September 1940 the allies were able to push them back into Libya. The Germans though had an agenda. They wanted to capture the Suez Canal, enter Palestine and start an Arab uprising, then link up with their forces that were moving south from southern Russia. So, by February 1941 they reinforced the Italians and drove the British back into Egypt. One hundred and fifty miles from Cairo, at El Alamein, the offensive was halted. Ensuing battles took place and by November, 1942 the Germans in defeat retreated to Libya and Tunisia. The agenda was crushed!

During the war the Jewish community in Cairo was very strong. The Egyptian government was not only afraid that the young men would gather together and cause trouble, they were fearful of an uprising. In reaction to their fear they took all the young men and put them in a camp as a means to control them.

As Aref's position in the community was high up, he and his three sons were taken there. Charles, a teenager at the time recounts, "My mother was allowed to visit once a day to bring us food and cigarettes. We were kept there for eight months."

When the war ended the Bochi's continued to live in Egypt except for Fredi who moved to Israel and Sami who attended school in France.

Once the British gave Egypt back to the Arabs the family no longer had a good life living there. Between 1950 and 1955 various family members left. Despite it being illegal to do so, Aref started sending money out of the country. Bahaya also sewed money into her clothes so when the time came for them to leave she could take as much with her as possible.

In 1955, Charles married Sara and subsequently she was given a French passport. Although born in Alexandria she initially had a Bulgarian passport as her father was from there. Her family had moved back and forth between Alexandria and Cairo. She recalls, "During the war years every time the air raid sirens went off I had to run into a shelter." Her parents, David and Nina, remained in Egypt for a long time until things got very bad and then they went to Israel where their other daughter Luna lived.

After their marriage, they, along with Aref and Bahaya moved to Paris, France. From there they all relocated to Villiers Leval which had a large Jewish community.

With the birth of their daughter Ghislaine, Charles and Sara decided to leave as there were too many people and not enough work. Given a choice between Australia and Canada, Sara said, "Let's go to

Canada as they speak French there." They would have had no trouble with languages though where ever they had decided to go as they were both multilingual. Charles spoke French, English, Hebrew, Ladino and Arabic. Sara spoke French, English, Ladino, Arabic, Spanish, Italian, and a little German and Greek.

They sailed to Canada on a ship. At first Charles found the country too cold so they returned to France. Twice more they journeyed back and forth. Finally in 1959 they stayed in Montreal permanently. Eventually, Sara's mother Nina and her sister, Luna with her family joined them from Israel. They called Canada, "the land of opportunity."

Charles had previously worked as an accountant for the American government and as a drycleaner. Unable to obtain employment in either of those fields his best friend suggested he work as a travel agent. In 1961 his father sent him $3000.00 to open a travel agency. This became the family business and his daughter, eventually took it over.

Ghislaine recalls, "As my parents were Egyptian I was brought up differently from most people in Montreal. When I was a teenager I remember having to explain to my friends why we did what we did, the food that we ate, and the traditions that we had. Also we were Sephardi and not Ashkenazi as were most Jews in Montreal at that time and we were not very religious.

My mother was a big influence in my life. She taught me to go with the flow, to accept changes. My father was very hard on me out of love. He made me the stronger person that I am today.

I feel that we should never forget what happened to the Jewish people during the war. It is very important to remember. It has made me strong in my beliefs."

# CHAPTER ELEVEN

## Hiding

T he Cohen and Leon families had lived in Thessaloniki, Greece
since 1492. They were part of the Sephardi community which had
fled the Spanish Inquisition.

When the Spanish Jews were expelled they were invited to settle in
lands controlled by the Ottoman Empire, which included Greece, Italy,
Turkey, and North Africa. The Ottomans were very tolerant religiously
and were well aware of the contributions that the Jews had made to
Spain financially, educationally and culturally. In 1821 Greece gained
its independence.

The other main group of Jewish people, the Romaniote community,
had existed there since antiquity and were integrated into Orthodox
Greek society.

By the turn of the century Thessaloniki was one-third Greek, one-
third Jewish and one-third Turkish. Everyone lived and prospered well.
It was a storybook tale of co-existence.

Elie Cohen, born in the early 1900's, had six sisters: Marie, Sol,
Lidia, Rachel, Matilde and Sarina. Their parents had passed away before
1939. Two of his sisters, Marie, the eldest, and Matilde lived with their
husbands and sons in Istanbul (Constantinople), Turkey. Elie managed
a movie theatre. He was well educated and spoke English and French.

Jeanne Leon was born nine years after Elie. Her parents were
Isaac and Henriette and she had six brothers and sisters: Rachel, Juda,
Jacques, Sara, Maurice and Berthe. There were two sides to the family

as after his first wife, Jamila, died Isaac married Henriette, Jamila's niece. They lived in a large house which included the in-laws.

All the children attended French school as it was the better institute. In addition to Ladino, French was the main language spoken at home during the day. English was also learned at school.

Isaac owned a soap factory, The Macedonian Industry of Soap, and a lot of real estate throughout the country.

Italy endeavoured to occupy Greece in October, 1940 but was stopped by the Greek army. To protect its ally Germany stepped in on April 6th, 1941 and the Bulgarians invaded the 20th. By June 1st all of Greece was taken over and divided into three zones with control going to the three conquerors. Since the King and the government had fled, a quisling Greek government was set up.

The Germans had entered Thessaloniki on April 9th. It came under German control on the 10th when the Greek military surrendered it to them.

In the beginning nothing was done against the Jews so the Leon family remained in the city.

On July 11, 1942 Jewish men between eighteen and forty-five were ordered by the Germans to register at Eleftherias Square. There they were subjected to humiliation and torture. They were also sent on forced labour assignments for Muller and Tod companies. The community paid a large sum of money to have the men released. This was the first warning of danger.

On December 6th the 2000 year old Jewish cemetery was demolished so that the ancient tombstones could be used to build sidewalks and walls. Jeanne said, "Not wanting the family to be desecrated, Jacques went to the cemetery and collected the bones of sixteen relatives. They were labeled and stored individually at the factory, in sacs used to sell soap."

By February, 1943 Jewish people were not allowed to work. Ordered to wear the yellow star the Leon's refused. They paid someone and obtained false identification documents that said they were Greek

Orthodox. Everyone changed their names to Greek ones. Jacques became Dimitrios Papadopulos and Maurice became Georgios Mavropulos.

On March 7th Jewish businesses were distributed to Greek custodians.

Then on March 25th all Jews were forced to live in ghettos. With this Jeanne and her family decided to flee as quickly as possible. They succeeded in getting to Athens which was under Italian control. It was fortunate that they had the foresight and capability to leave.

Jacques though, did not leave immediately. Giorgios Mitzeliotis, who sold the family olive oil for the soap used at the factory and was their friend, came to his rescue. He took Jacques by boat to the island of Skopelos, where he lived. He and his wife Magdalini were Orthodox Christians and he was the village headsman.

Elie and Jeanne married in June and the two families were now united.

On September 8th, with the downfall of Italy, the Germans took control over their zone, which included Athens, and focused their attention on the Jews that were there.

The Grand Rabbi of Athens, Elias Barzilai, was told to give a list of names, addresses and assets to the Department of Jewish Affairs. Instead of doing this he destroyed the community's records and advised people to either go into hiding or run away.

At the same time the Archbishop of Athens, Damaskinos, requested that his priests and their congregations help the Jews. Despite the threat of imprisonment many Orthodox Christians did just that and risking their lives hid people in their homes.

The Leon family was no longer safe so Giorgios came to their rescue. He travelled to Evia, where they had gone after leaving Athens, and brought them to Skopelos. In all, he hid fourteen family members: Isaac and Henriette, Jacques, Maurice, Berthe, Jeanne and Elie, Sarina (Elie's sister), Juda and his wife Victoria and their children Nina and

Isaac, Solomon Molho (Victoria's brother), and Isaac Rousso (Solomon's friend).

Jeanne said, "It was a stark existence on the island of Skopelos." The group was split up and hidden in two small huts in the mountains that were used by the villagers during nut gathering season. Three times a week, Magdalini and Giorgios, or his brother-in-law Mr. Korfiatis and his wife and daughters brought the family food.

When the Germans came to search the island the local Greek Orthodox priest, with a gun hidden under his cassock, made the trip on foot to the two huts to pray with them and to bring them food and news. That was the only way that they had any news of what was going on between the two groups and in the world. They couldn't risk being outside all the time as there was a danger of being turned in so they had to hide during the day.

Jeanne's sister Rachel, her husband Albert and their son Sam went into hiding in Athens. Her other sister, Sara along with her husband Sam and their daughter Lola were taken out by the British as he held a Maltese passport. First taken to Athens they then went to Palestine.

Elie's sister, Sol, her husband and daughter Lilian also hid in Athens. Another sister, Rachel, with her husband and daughter Mona, managed to escape through Turkey to Palestine. His other sister, Lidia, whose husband had been a member of parliament and died before the war, and her daughter, Ninon, were sent to Auschwitz.

By the time Greece was liberated in October, 1944 the Jewish community was almost completely exterminated. Thessaloniki had the highest percentage of people killed.

On the island of Skopelos the Leon family remained hidden for about a year. They were able to survive as did Rachel and Sol with their families who had been hiding in Athens. Sadly Lidia and Ninon perished.

The Leons returned to Thessaloniki. During the war their home had been taken over as well as all the land that they owned. The assets of everyone who had died in the concentration camps went to the Jewish Community of Thessaloniki and it was very wealthy. Unfortunately for the Leon family their things were never given to the Community but were taken over by the government. Sixty years later, they are still fighting to get all their assets back which include a piece of land that is a major park.

Economically it was quite difficult for the family. Two of the brothers reopened the soap factory as they had managed to get it back. This led to the discovery that during the war a Greek person had gone to the factory and wanting to use the sacs that the soap was sold in, dumped all the bones that Jacques had collected, into one box. After finding them they were reburied together in a grave with all their names inscribed on the tombstone.

The factory though was not enough to support everyone. So, another brother opened a bicycle and motorcycle parts shop in partnership with his brother-in-law. One sister married a wealthy man who made clay roof tiles. Elie managed a movie theatre.

In 1957, having had a tough time financially, Jeanne and Elie decided to leave. Jeanne, "Wanting to be near someone we knew we applied to both the USA and Canada. My sister's husband's aunt lived in Montreal." Elie's best friend Marcel Nadjary, who had survived Auschwitz, lived in New York.

With quotas for immigration they were slated to go to either Detroit or Montreal. Acceptance from Canada came first. Having paid $815.00 for the family in steerage they arrived in Halifax on the ship, SS Queen Fredericka with their children Helen and Henry. From there they took the train to Montreal. The Baron de Hirsch Organization had set up an apartment for them in the neighbourhood of Snowdon and helped Elie find a job.

Elie worked as a book-keeper for the Ace Office Equipment store and Jeanne was a home maker. Sadly, nine years after their arrival, he passed away.

After this Jeanne wanted to return to Greece but decided to stay as she felt that educationally and job-wise, there were more opportunities in Canada for her children. It was a difficult decision for her to make, but in the end she felt that she had made the right one. It was a very brave thing for her to do.

Henry said, "My mother was a bigger influence on my life than my father as I was so young when he died. She was a very strong person and it was self-sacrificing to do what she did. She gave me a sense of family and responsibility to my children. She was bright, funny, well read and gave me an interest in languages and books."

In 2009 Henry returned to Greece. His family there are very active in the Jewish community. A cousin in Athens, Isaac Leon, managed to get a little park at the foot of the acropolis and built a Jewish memorial. Henry says, "My parents shared with me what it was like during the war. I am proud of my family for having the capability to save themselves and figuring out how to do it. They found a way to make it happen."

Giorgios Mitzeliotis has been described as a brave man and a good Christian. The Mitzeliotis and Korfiatis families were named Righteous Gentiles by Yad Vasham in Israel and are named in the Holocaust Museum in Israel and New York.

After the war Marcel Nadjary stayed with the Leon family. He had been good friends with Elie Cohen and Maurice Leon. Later Marcel's daughter Nellie married Maurice Leon's son. Twenty-five years ago, while doing construction at Auschwitz, Marcel Nadjary's leather knapsack which contained his diary was dug up. It has now been translated into many languages. It contains drawings of the ovens and other things.

1937 - Wedding of Sara Leon and Sam Amariglio.

Front row: Third from left, Sam; second from right Berthe. Middle row in front of bride: Henriette and Isaac. Third row: far left, Rachel, Albert, Victoria, Juda; beside bride, Jacques; bride and groom Sara and Sam. Maurice and Jeanne are behind the groom.

L-R: Elie Cohen, Berthe Leon, Jeanne Cohen, Betty Siaky, Sam Leon and his wife Riri and Maurice Leon. Front: Eddy Siacky

Marcel Nadjary and Maurice Leon

ISRAELITISCHE KULTUSGEMEINDE SALONIKI
ΙΣΡΑΗΛΙΤΙΚΗ ΚΟΙΝΟΤΗΣ ΘΕΣΣΑΛΟΝΙΚΗΣ

# PERSONAL - AUSWEIS
## ΔΕΛΤΙΟΝ ΤΑΥΤΟΤΗΤΟΣ

Registernummer                                    6520
'Αριθ. μητρώου
Familienname        Leon
'Επώνυμον
Name                        Jacob
"Ονομα
Name des Vaters oder des Gatten        Isac
"Ονομα πατρός ή συζύγου
Geburtsjahr        1910
"Ετος γεννήσεως
Beruf        Εμπορ
'Επάγγελμα
Adresse
Διεύθυνσις
        Saloniki den        1943
'Εν Θεσ)νίκη τῇ

DER PRÄSIDENT DER ISRAELITISCHEN KULTUSGEMEINDE
Ο ΠΡΟΕΔΡΟΣ ΤΗΣ ΙΣΡΑΗΛΙΤΙΚΗΣ ΚΟΙΝΟΤΗΤΟΣ

Getl. Gen. No. 2788 B

Jacques Leon's identity card

Jacques Leon's yellow star has the same
number as on his identity card.

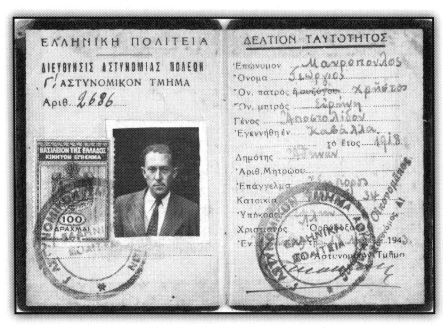

Maurice Leon's false identity card

Maurice Leon's false name – Georgios Mavropulos

Georgios Mizeliotis

As the cemetery had been desecrated in 1942,
this tomb stone was made after the war.

# CHAPTER TWELVE

## On the Move

**M**oise and Sarina Beza, their son Sabetai and daughter Yvette lived in Thessaloniki, Greece.

Yvette was a child when the 1940-41 bombing raids occurred on the city. She said, "I will remember that all my life." Moise felt his family would be safer in the village of Vysitsa up in the mountain near Volos, so they moved there. He returned to Thessaloniki to look after his business and visited them every now and then.

On one occasion, after waiting a few days for Moise to come, a villager told Sarina, "Do not wait any longer." Moise had been taken prisoner by the Germans and was placed in the Eptapyrghion prison. With this news Sarina moved back to Salonika. She intervened for his release at the Kommandatur and brought letters with her from three German industrialists that said, "Moise is a good customer." After ninety three days of imprisonment, during which time the Germans collected prisoners to be executed as penalties for sabotage made by the partisans, he was released.

In February, 1943 they had to wear the yellow star on their clothes.

In March, Jewish people were forced out of their homes and into the Syngrou, Miaouli and Baron Hirsch ghettos which had been set up.

The Beza's moved to the Syngrou ghetto to Sarina's aunt's house. They were only able to take the essentials with them. Yvette said, "My father tried to get us out of there."

One of Moise's acquaintances, Mr. Gaspar Gasparian, found a German military truck driver, who for a considerable amount of gold coins would take them to the city of Lamia, which was under Italian control. Yvette recalls, "The German driver did not keep his word and made us get out in Katerini, which was under German rule. We had no choice but to return to Thessaloniki since we did not have any documents with us."

Yvette remembers, "Several days later, Mr. Gasparian came to our home at ten o'clock at night and said, "You must leave quickly with me." He had been told that the Germans would come for them in the morning. His actions helped save them as at daybreak all the people in the ghetto were transported by train to Auschwitz.

They then moved to the country ghetto where Yvette's grandmother, Myrou, and Sarina's sisters Rachel and Estrea lived. Moise was still trying to find a way to get his family out of the city.

One day he found a friend of his, Lazaros Kosmidis, on the road, who asked him, "Why are you still here Moise?" He replied, "I did not find a way to leave." Lazaros said, "I will come in the afternoon to take you with me to my house in Saranda Ekklisies."

So that nobody in the neighborhood would see them, they hid in his home. They were there for fifteen days. During this time Lazaros helped them get false identification cards with Christian names. They borrowed the names of another friendly family, the Papaiconomos, and became Vasilios, Victoria, Miltos and Frosso.

Unable to stay any longer in Thessaloniki because it was occupied by the Germans they left the city. For the next two years they were constantly on the move, from place to place.

They journeyed to Kozani on a gazozen and from there trekked by mules through the mountains to Larissa which was under Italian control. Later they went by truck to Athens where they stayed with some relatives in Marousi. Fearful of the Germans coming they left.

They then went to Ioannina and remained there for a while, hiding in a house. When the Germans commandeered some of the rooms in the courtyard, in order to use them as a kitchen for their officers, they decided it was not safe to stay there anymore either.

Sarina who knew how to speak Italian went to the Carabinierie and said, "I was born an Italian and would like permission to travel out of Greece to Albania to stay with my husband's brother, Ino." Permission was granted. The family journeyed first to Dirrachio (Durres), and then to Tirana. With Italy's surrender the Germans took control over Albania. When the Allies began bombing raids on Tirana they had to be on the move yet again.

This time they tried to cross the Ionian Sea, on a barge, in order to reach southern Italy as it was held by the Allies. Yvette said, "Half way across the sea, due to bad weather, the barge sunk and we nearly drowned. Our good fortune helped us as we were rescued by a boat."

Once in Italy they were put on a big steamer ship with thousands of Allied soldiers that were headed to Alexandria, Egypt. When they arrived they were taken to a refugee camp in the Sinai dessert at the Moses Wells. There they lived in tents with about three thousand other Greeks. After eight months they went to Cairo under the protection of the exiled Greek government where they remained for an additional eight months.

Upon the liberation of Greece in October, 1944 they returned to live in Thessaloniki.

Yvette said, "We found out that all our relatives had died except for three of my cousins who had survived the death camps." Yvette's grandmother Myrou and Sarina's sisters, Rachel and Estrea, perished in Auschwitz together with their families as did Sarina's other sisters and brothers. Every one of Sarina's thirty-three family members was deceased. Yvette comments, "We never recovered from the scars the Holocaust left in our souls. Even today we burst into tears when we read or hear something about the death camps."

In 1956, Yvette married Maurice Leon. In 1965, they moved to Athens.

Yvette Beza with her parents Moise and
Sarina and her brother Sabetai.

Yvette Beza

# CHAPTER THIRTEEN

## *Survival*

The Lowy's lived an idealistic life in the small village of Balassagyarmat, Hungary. They were medical doctors and quite affluent. They had two daughters, one of whom was Eva. She was born in the mid 1920's, and spoke both Hungarian and German.

In 1940 Hungary became a member of the Axis powers and in 1941 took part in the invasion of the Soviet Union and Yugoslavia.

While fighting against the Soviet Union, Hungary was involved in secret peace negotiations with the United States and the United Kingdom. When Hitler discovered this, in March of 1944, German forces occupied Hungary. SS Colonel Adolf Eichmann then went there and oversaw the deportation of Jewish people to Auschwitz-Birkenau concentration camp.

Eva, and her parents and sister, were rounded up and taken by train to Auschwitz. When they arrived her father was separated from them.

As she was fluent in German she was put to work in an office at the camp. Cruelty however existed there. Eva said, "One guard liked to put out his cigarettes on my lips."

For food everyone was given a daily ration of a slice of bread. One lady at the camp, who was fairly wealthy, had managed to smuggle in a very expensive diamond ring. She wanted to exchange it with someone for their bread but found no takers. Eva said, "My sister, mother, and I contemplated chipping in one of our slices and we would then share our remaining ones. However, after debating it we decided not to. Our bread was more valuable than the ring."

Almost all the Hungarian Jews that had arrived at Auschwitz-Birkenau concentration camp were killed immediately upon their arrival. It is presumed that Eva's father was one of them, as he was never seen or heard from again, but there is no way of knowing this with certainty.

For a while her mother and sister managed to stay alive. Her mother though died there. Her sister survived until the end of the war but did not live long afterwards as she had contracted tuberculosis. Unable to get antibiotics in time, as there was a short supply, she died in a hospital in Germany.

Eva remained at Auschwitz until she was liberated. The fact that she spoke German and was able to surreptitiously steal garbage like potato peels, for a few additional calories enabled her to survive.

When the war ended in 1945 the Russians were in Hungary. After they took over, no one had a home. Whatever property Eva's family had was confiscated. This was a very dark time. Deprivation was everywhere and anti-Semitism was very much so.

Eva did not return to Balassagyarmat as there was nothing to return to. Instead she went to Budapest. She was adopted by a loving, older couple who became her surrogate parents. Dafi, which was not his real name but an endearing Hungarian name, was Jewish and his wife was not.

# CHAPTER FOURTEEN

## False Identification Papers

Ferenc and Maria Klein lived in Budapest, Hungary with their son, Ervin, who was born in the early 1920's. Their surname was changed to Kallos when there was a movement in Hungary to change all Germanic names to make them sound more Hungarian. Ervin now went by this new name.

For the first few years of the war most Jewish people were protected from deportation to German concentration camps. They were however, subjected to a series of anti-Jewish laws. These laws prevented them from participating in economic and public life. Ervin, who was Jewish, had been a medical student in another city. Ervin said, "Under those laws I was no longer allowed to study at the university and was forced to leave school."

Ervin had a friend that he had known since high school who was a printer. To help the Kallos family hide their Jewish identity he not only printed false identification papers for them but for many other people.

During this time you had to either serve in the war or work in a Hungarian labour camp. Ervin chose the latter. The camps had soccer teams that were rivals with each other. As he was an athlete and a skilled soccer player, Ervin had it easy. He said, "As a valued member of the team I received somewhat preferential treatment." He was very fortunate. However, had his true identity been discovered he would have been killed.

Even though they had ration cards, Ervin used to sneak away from the camp to find more food for his mother. He took the train, often sitting just on planks, into the country side to scour for something to eat.

There were times when he had to try to outsmart the Red Arrows, who were Hungary's version of the German Brown Shirts. One time when he wasn't carrying his identity papers, they stopped him. As a bluff he offered to show them that he wasn't circumcised so they could see he wasn't Jewish. Ervin said, "Come in the alley and I'll show you." It seemed like he was almost calling the other guy a homosexual if he were to look so they let him go. They would not risk any suspicion of being a homosexual as it would have meant they would be sent to a concentration camp.

Thanks to the false identification papers Ervin and his parents survived the war. Maria's brother also survived but other members of the family did not.

Ervin continued to live in Budapest. He tried to go back to medical school but ended up becoming a business man of sorts in dental supplies.

In the early 1950's Ervin met Eva Lowy and they got married. In 1956 while vacationing in Austria the Hungarian Revolution broke out. Although it was not successful it allowed for a brief window when the borders were relaxed and people were able to sneak out. They went back to Hungary, got their son Garry, and returned to Austria. They left with only a knapsack and spent the next eight to nine months in a refugee camp.

They applied to go to the U.S.A. because they had family there but could not get in because the quota for Hungarians was full. They then tried to go to Canada. Once accepted, they flew to Montreal in 1957. They lived in the neighbourhood of Snowdon.

Life was very difficult for them when they arrived. They were immigrants with no English language skills. People they knew got help from Jewish agencies but when Ervin, with hat in hand, asked for help from the Combined Jewish Appeal agency, he was turned away. They were starving with a baby to feed and when they went again they were given $10.00. Ervin had friends who had been given furnished apartments but that didn't happen for them. It appeared that if you had connections you got help and Ervin didn't have them.

Eva got a job doing machine work at Marconi. Eventually she got work as a draftsman and then worked at an office as a payroll clerk where she stayed until she retired.

Ervin's first job was as a dishwasher and then he got a job as a shipper at a toy distributor. Even though they were quite poor he was able to get toys at a discount for his son. Garry remembers, "I didn't feel poor as I had good toys." Ervin then became a toy wholesaler. In the early 1960's he became an insurance man and created a business which his son eventually took over.

Both Ervin and Garry were protective of Eva as she suffered from what she had experienced during the war. Although she would not talk about her time in Auschwitz she would volunteer an anecdote here and there.

Ervin would not allow any reference to the war years and there was a silence imposed on the past. It was a taboo subject and he would not permit Garry to ask Eva anything about it. In their home no concentration camp war movies were watched while Eva was alive. Ervin though, would sometimes talk to Garry about his experiences.

Of his childhood Garry remembers that it had been good. He was the centre of his parent's universe. He says, "I grew up with European sensibilities and was a little bit removed from Canadian culture. My parents had a big influence on everything in my life". He further recalls, "They gave me guidance and supported me throughout university as much as they could. They were also supportive of my athletic ability and my father would come out to watch me wrestle. They were huge fans."

Garry won gold at the Quebec provincial level. He was an Olympian and was on the Canadian Olympic 1980 and 1984 wrestling teams.

# CHAPTER FIFTEEN

## Deported

Isaak and Regina Goldstein lived in Gonc, Hungary. They had four sons: Zoltan, Imre, Lazslo, another son and a daughter, Jolan. Family meant everything to Jolan and she was very close to her brothers.

Isaak was a well off land owner. The family was Jewish. They were very religious and kept a kosher kitchen.

At the beginning of the war Jolan had been studying to be a doctor but was forced to leave medical school under the anti-Jewish laws. She spoke English, German, Hungarian and Slovak.

When the Nazis took over the country in 1944, she was in her twenties. She and her brothers did not look Jewish. When she wore the yellow star she would be asked, "Why are you wearing that star, as you aren't Jewish?" She would reply, "I am."

She had several chances to escape but wanted to stay with her family. When her parents, who looked Jewish, were rounded up, she and her brothers remained with them. The Germans asked, "Why are you going with them as none of you look Jewish?" Refusing to be separated they were deported along with them.

Jolan and Regina were put on a train to Theresienstadt. Upon their arrival she went into one line and her mother another. Isaak and his four sons were taken to a different place.

For the next year and a half Jolan was in three different camps: Theresienstadt, Bergen-Belsen and then Auschwitz. In one of the camps she was a labourer building planes.

While in the camps there were a few people with whom she made friends with. She said, "It was people who stuck together that survived."

Food was scarce. Whatever food she was able to scrounge she shared with other people. She also tried to save some for her brothers thinking that if she ever found them that she would give it to them.

Between two of the camps she survived the "death march". This was a forced walk to move prisoners from camps near the advancing war fronts to those inside Germany. With insufficient food supplies people were weakened. They were also demoralized as conditions were harsh and brutal. If one did not keep up they were executed by being shot.

Of her time in the camps, Jolan, to this day says, "I don't know how I survived." As for her mother, after they had been split up, she never heard from her again.

After the war Jolan met Alexander Grodan.

Alexander had been born into a farming family in Kosice, Czechoslovakia. His family were secular and Jewish in name only.

He had seven brothers and one sister. His parents were determined that all their children would get a good education. As a result his siblings were engineers and lawyers. Alexander was a doctor. He spoke several languages including English, German, French, Italian, Slovak and Hungarian.

In 1939 when the Germans took complete control of his country he was thirty years old and in the army. He was rounded up and sent to an internment camp and because he was a doctor he remained there.

Jolan and Alexander lived in Kosice, Czechoslovakia. They married and had two children. She studied at the university and worked in a chemistry lab. He was a brain surgeon.

When the country became a Soviet satellite state in 1948, Jolan wanted to be free and to not live in a communist country. She also wanted to be with her three brothers who had survived the war. Two had gone to live in Montreal. The third was in Vienna, Austria. He was educated at the Sorbonne and was a doctor.

In 1964, Alexander saved the wife of a very high official. He told Alexander, "If there is anything I can do for you, let me know." Jolan, who had been trying to leave for a long time said, "Yes, there is something you can do for us." The official got them a visa to go on vacation to Hungary. Once there, her brother from Vienna came and took them back to Austria. They left with only the clothes on their backs. After staying there for three months they received Canadian visas and flew to Montreal.

Their daughter, Susan said, "Life was tough at home. My best years were when my father was alive." Alexander passed when she was young.

Jolan spoke frequently with Susan about her war-time experiences. There was a sense of guilt though in their conversations as she wanted her to know what she had sacrificed for her. Susan said, "My mother was very strict with me. She loved me but she was also self-centered. I had to understand her but she did not have to understand me. Everything that had been taken away from her when she was growing up, she wanted me to do. This included becoming a doctor. When I stopped my medical studies to get married she was furious."

Despite all of that, Susan says, "I am grateful to my mother as she made me very strong and tough. Also thanks to her I have a very close relationship with my own children."

Susan is thankful her parents survived the Holocaust.